In and Out of the Horse Latitudes

poems by

Mary Imo-Stike

Finishing Line Press
Georgetown, Kentucky

In and Out of the Horse Latitudes

*To my father, J. Francis Imo,
who kept our stories.*

Copyright © 2018 by Mary Imo-Stike
ISBN 978-1-63534-455-4 First Edition
All rights reserved under International and Pan-American Copyright Conventions. No part of this book may be reproduced in any manner whatsoever without written permission from the publisher, except in the case of brief quotations embodied in critical articles and reviews.

ACKNOWLEDGMENTS

The following poems have appeared in these journals or on-line journals. Some were earlier versions of what is here, and some have my maiden name (Mary Susan Imo) as their by-line.

Young Ravens Review ~ "Women Grounded by Work" (as "Florence and Delia"); "I Hear Her Songs with the Scent of Lilacs" (as "The Hit Songs of 1953"); "Boiling Point"
Mountain Ink ~ "Cabbage Roses"
Antietam Review ~ "Stain" (as "The Stain")
Phoebe ~ "He Gives Me His Bigger Space"
Earth's Daughters ~ "In and Out of the Horse Latitudes"
Connotation Press, an Online Artifact ~ "Poem Inspired by James Wright's Fear of Working in the Glass Plant"; "Far from Home"
Picaroon Poetry ~ "My Coat with Rainbow Sleeves"

Publisher: Leah Maines
Editor: Christen Kincaid
Cover Art: Randi Ward
Author Photo: Randi Ward
Cover Design: Elizabeth Maines McCleavy

Printed in the USA on acid-free paper.
Order online: www.finishinglinepress.com
also available on amazon.com

Author inquiries and mail orders:
Finishing Line Press
P. O. Box 1626
Georgetown, Kentucky 40324
U. S. A.

Table of Contents

Women Grounded by Work ... 1

I Hear Her Songs with the Scent of Lilacs ... 3

I Wanted More ... 4

The Permanence of Trees ... 5

Boiling Point ... 6

Through an Open Window ... 7

Cabbage Roses ... 9

A Time of Pines ... 10

Stain ... 12

He Gives Me His Bigger Space ... 14

Homing ... 15

Still Not Far from Yasgur's Farm ... 17

The Apprentice Plumber Walks Home from Trade School ... 19

Building: Denver ... 20

In and Out of the Horse Latitudes ... 24

My River Life ... 26

The Language of Men ... 27

Poem Inspired by James Wright's Fear of Working in the
   Glass Plant ... 29

My Coat with Rainbow Sleeves ... 31

Far from Home ... 32

Women Grounded by Work

I am grown from women
grounded by work.

My Grandma Florence left the family farm
in Addison, New York in 1917
to live in Rochester.
The first winter her father
brought her a box of potatoes
for comfort and survival.
She worked in factories, munitions, then perfume,
and as a clerk in McCurdy's department store
and later at the Rochester Post Office.
She was proud of her brass Post Office pin
a pony express carrier, the steed's legs fashioned wide
in full gallop, the boyish rider with his wide felt hat
and leather shoulder bag.
She wore it pinned high on her broad fronted housedress,
or on a hand knit cardigan sweater.

My father's mother Delia
was sent by her father from their home
on the Tonawanda reservation,
to Carlisle Indian School.
He was a track laborer on the New York Central Railroad,
had no way to care for his children when their mother died
giving birth to Delia.
As a young teenager, she came to the city
to work as a domestic with her girlfriend Evelyn TwoGuns.
They kept house and cared for the children
of the rich white families on St. Paul Boulevard.

At family dinners
Florence and Delia told us stories
of those hard first years in Rochester,
before Grandpa Frederick came to be an auto worker
or Grandpa John drove his hack for weddings and funerals.

And now, my life,
a shrine to these women
in sepia-toned
photos in golden oak frames.

I say their names,
set my stubby candle before them.
Florence uses her kitchen shears to trim the wick,
Delia's strong brown fingers strike the match

and they light the flame.

I Hear Her Songs with the Scent of Lilacs

The back door stood open all the day,
wispy breezes passing in through the screen
and rushing across the kitchen floor.
My mother might be in the basement cool
doing laundry, upstairs straightening bedrooms
or sitting with a cup of coffee
on the back steps.

Our kitchen was awash
with Arthur Godfrey or the soaps on the radio.
I was napping but still able to hear
the consistent hum of her latest favorite song,
The Tennessee Waltz or Perry Como's
Don't Let the Stars Get in Your Eyes.

Her music was a promise of a good day,
a loving blanket pulled carefully
up and over my sleepy self.

Her routine of joy held me,
furrowed deep and unmoving,
an anchor that I would never lose.
I still do my morning chores
with the radio on, singing,
an echo of her contented essence,
strong and sweet and pretty.

She passed her star to my eye,
the eye she shaped to see the world.
I hear her songs with the scent of lilacs,
oil soap or line-dried cotton clothes;
I breathe deeply and
feel her presence in the legion
of mothers we all carry.

I Wanted More

My father wore a plaid flannel shirt,
buttoned to the collar, on winter Saturdays.
Sometimes he made our supper,
spaghetti with his meat sauce,
onions and peppers, chopped fine,
mushrooms sliced thin and floating
in the spice-fragrant simmer.
I played with my sister,
coloring on a card table set up in the living room.
We waited for Mom to come home from Grandma's,
carrying a loaf of crusty bread.

Later we played outside
and the frigid night air slapping at my cheeks
told me of another world outside my comfort.
There were glimpses of it
when an unfamiliar car rolled down our street,
the dash lights revealing a brief look
at the face of a stranger, scowling in concentration
to navigate the snowy street
or yelling at his kids in the backseat
while taking a quick drag from his cigarette.

I saw more when peeping in
at neighbors, in their private rooms,
innocently illuminated for me,
crouched in the bushes, holding my breath,
transformed by my imagination
to a possibility of being a kid of another home,
one with different people,
who told and laughed at jokes I'd never heard
followed unusual traditions and routines.

Written in my family's roots is the strength
that pushed me out, encouraged curiosity,
told me to seek and see all that's there,
to get closer to the edge of what's familiar.

I sucked in the strange air until my chest burned
and still wanted more.

The Permanence of Trees

We lived in a city in a forest,
huge American Elms lined our street.
In my imagination, we were forest folk,
I was a tree girl.
At age four, I knew our trees
swaying their bushy tresses
made the wind. At eight,
the exposed roots
where the sidewalk and our driveway came together
made a tiny medieval manor land, terraced farm fields
in among plots for family homes,
moat banks close to the wide trunked castle.
The hump of tree base that faced the sidewalk
was the cathedral, perfectly placed in the center of things
with a dark entryway.
The grass that grew out along the curb line—pastureland.
I imagined that on holidays, the entire population sauntered
down the root-bound roads
to gather in the fields for feasting and dancing.

One spring day, a huge spray truck,
from the city's parks department fleet
rolled down the street
spraying a poison on each treetop
to protect it from Dutch Elm Disease.
Those of us kids playing outside that day
ran onto our front porch and huddled together
until it passed, afraid to look but peeking
at the monstrous metal tube that swiveled
to face one side of the street
then the other and belch a cloudy, stinky spray
onto upper limbs and branches
then roar away to the next block.

The scent of the poison lingered;
we were called inside for the remainder of the day.
Seeing my forest invaded,
I learned to protect and hide the things I love
from the bigger world;
that what I cherish is not always safe.
Even the permanence of trees
was threatened.

Boiling Point

At fourteen, I read Steinbeck, Salinger,
John Knowles' *A Separate Peace*,
searched graveyards for history
and started drinking coffee.

That was the summer of race riots in our city,
1964. Days and nights of fighting, curfew and looting,
I could hear the sirens through
the open window in my bedroom all night.
At home we were restless, on edge, waiting
and watchful like before a thunderstorm
that promises severity and damage in its fury.

The riots erupted, forcing us to become aware
of what we had avoided, refused to see
on the slummy streets Dad would not drive
after dark, or if he had to, he would say,
"Girls, lock your doors."
The simmer of discontent heated up,
and boiled over for three days, its stink
covering the city, it entered the forced-open windows
of our houses we had thought were safe,
surrounded our supper table where we talked of nothing else.
How could this happen here? What does it mean?
Is it that bad here, like the South?
And we knew it was wretched
in the black neighborhoods
that we held so far away from our existence.
Yeah, we saw the poverty, but could not fathom
its desperation.

My education that summer:
not stories of the Okies in the 30's or spoiled adolescent boys
in prep school, so fascinating but foreign to me;
in my hometown, the storm was rumbling
up and down the streets and through our walls.
We could not escape or hide our knowledge
anymore.
Our whole family came of age.

Through An Open Window, Rochester, NY, 1965

She is there at seven when I ride by
on the city bus on my way to school.
The heavy black woman running the steam ironing machine
at East Main Linen Service,
visible through the street level window
in the gritty brick building.
The bus stops there.
Rush-hour traffic back-up lets me
leave my fifteen-year-old world in that moment
and imagine being in her place,
sweating that much so early in the day,
her mouth open in laughter
at a joke called out by an unseen coworker.
I visualize going where she lives
on the other side of town, so foreign to me,
dealing with her man and kids,
maybe sharing a quart of beer with her sister Friday nights
ironing clothes in the hot kitchen
while the old man watches the fights on TV.

That is where I want to be,
where her bed sheets crisp and ghostly white
take her worn-out body
the nights her young ones sleep through
and there be no need to hold her breath
when her man stirs and turns slowly toward her.
She swallows her craving for rest,
a peaceful respite
with the whiskey taste in his mouth.

This is the passion I do not see at home
in our tidy neighborhood of old but well-cared for houses
where our family tries so hard
to be more like the families on the next street up the hill,
closer to the serene Highland Park,
farther from the noise of South Clinton Avenue.
We proudly label ourselves "middle class",
in our minds a step above the fate of our grandfather
who worked in the carburetor plant.
My parents send us to Catholic school
with discipline that insures a ticket to college

and release from ever having to sweat
working on a factory floor.

Any outward expression
would cheapen our appearance,
threaten our position,
push us closer to the clear,
invisible line between us
and residents of the inner city,
too loud and raw,
like the Black Madonna I long to be
whose feeling flowers from her pores
like the sweat on her arms,
tiny beads blossoming together
beneath her cheap white cotton uniform blouse,
and high on her brow
below the Linen Service cap
so close to me but just beyond
what I will ever really see.

Cabbage Roses

I feared that I hung up the telephone
just as my grandmother was answering.
She would wonder who was calling,
if anything was wrong,
on such a cold night.

I had dialed the heavy black phone beside my parents' bed,
but no answer after many rings, the empty echoes
called me to visualize where their phone sits on the desk,
in their dining room, so warm with their presence,
the quiet, measured, scheduled existence
of my Protestant, working-class grandparents,
who were always home.
Grandpa should be reading in his rocker,
or listening to the radio,
an arm's length from the desk, from the ringing phone.
The huge, maternal cabbage roses on the wallpaper,
throughout the living and dining rooms,
heavy-headed, leaning in, keeping him safe.

But tonight the phone denied me peace of mind
gave me nothing but cold dead silence
reminded me of the fragility and swiftness
of life, and the permanence of loss
how we depend on someone staying in the places
our heart knows to find them.

When I put the receiver back on the cradle
I thought I heard her voice, small and expectant
but I hung up, then wondered if she was really there,
if she sat down again in the room of cabbage roses,
did I cross her mind on that lonely winter night?

A Time of Pines

The lowest widest boughs of the Eastern White Pines
in our neighborhood park
touched the ground after a hard snow
and formed a dry and softly bedded place
from the trunk outward
where we used to hide away.
In this natural secret chamber
where no wind blew,
we were invisible to anyone who passed.

We were younger than trees,
two Catholic high school kids
first-timers in lust that winter
in our private groundling's nest
late Sunday afternoons,
his damp coat beneath me, the scent
of wool and pine swirling together
like the milk in hot chocolate
I'd have when I got home.

Looking up, I absorbed
the strange beauty of this boy,
in love with me, surrounded by a myriad of limbs,
married to their core and all the rustic twigs
and spicy needles crowding around.
My thoughts often strayed to how much easier
the mechanics of life and love for boys,
like peeing: so unexposed, one zip and quickly done,
much less a risk, all around.

This holy place
was as removed from my daily life
of family, Church and school
as right from wrong.

I teetered between two worlds
knowing that the human thing we did beneath the trees
was wrong
but I was not,
and that I would not stop.

On the way home, he'd walk me
to the corner of my street,
and I would make up songs from the crunching music
our boot soles made on the snow packed sidewalk.

Stain

I worried about blood on my clothes,
on the back of my skirt
from sitting in stale classrooms
on dim and stuffy winter afternoons;
like the stain of genocide
but never hidden, it grew and spread
coming to full light on the East Main Street bus,
beneath the boundary of my coat's coverage.
Unmistakable, unforgivable, the worst stain,
it defied all my pretense, the hiding, covering,
being pure, being good and a girl
from Mercy High School
whose parents paid tuition
so she could attend with the suburban girls,
the daughters of dentists and lawyers.
I rode two city buses a day in the slush to get there
and they saw me bleeding like a slut.

My shame spread like the stain.
I'd laughed and pretend it didn't matter,
hoped for the day I'd be thirty-years old
and living in the suburbs, too,
with a professor husband
who wears hunter green sweaters
and sons who need me.
I dreamed of driving a car with leather seats
so I'd never worry
about the blood.

My life has given me struggle
and the wisdom that there is no cause for blood shame,
an insidious tool of the patriarchy,
that kept me unconfident, doubtful of my worth,
unbeautiful and repressed,
stuck in the place they picked for me.

Now I whisper across time
to the girl on the bus.
*"Claim your life, your blood.
Love your bright and dark*

*oddly shaped, conspicuous,
magnificent
Stain!"*

He Gives Me His Bigger Space

I see my father changing a car battery,
it's heavy and the acid is poison,
it can burn through his leather gloves or hobnail boots.
He sets it on the scrubby grass on the west side of the driveway
by the fence alongside the Japanese crabapple.
It's only just springtime, but he wears no jacket
and his always-tan biceps are hefty but soft
like unbaked wheat loaves waiting
to rise in tins on top of the stove,
under a gingham dishtowel.

He tells me stories of his childhood,
of the apartment on Joseph Avenue
where he sat alone waiting for his mother to get home from work;
of Sunday drives with his dad exploring all parts of his corner of the state.
He has a workbench of tools that call my name;
a top dresser drawer holding his neat Daddy stuff:
French cuff links, folded handkerchiefs,
a Saint Christopher medal, a money clip,
a black and silver rosary
and the warm and sintered scent of cedar and bay rum.
Like a lullaby, his golden baritone rehearses
the ancient antiphons of the Latin Mass.

Watching him, listening to his stories
connects me to why I am the person I am.
Years later I travelled far still carrying
talismans from home:
bone china teacups, a corn husk false face and beaded moccasins.
I picked up my own tools,
swung a pickaxe and shoveled railroad ballast.

I am still the seedling watching my father,
I am the thirsty ground soaking him up.
I always try to swim upstream with him,
into his bigger space of being.

Homing

We drove some miles
onto the reservation
that cool Spring morning
in 1974
our long hair, chestnutty,
our denim jackets with round brassy buttons
our embroidered collars on faded blue workshirts
our yellow brown work shoes from the Sears on Monroe Avenue.
We had Army surplus gunners' bags for purses.
Our high cheekbones flushed rosy.
Less than sixty miles from home
the Tonawanda Reservation
was worlds away.
We had visited so seldom
never before alone.
Now my sister and I
came upon that flat and ugly,
unwanted land
looking for a way
to be at home there.

We found Ella and Harrison Ground,
our grandma's sister and her husband,
in their plain clapboard house
stark center on a nondescript lot,
dead car beside the shrub-covered outbuilding,
a pale green glider on the front porch
and an old dog
suddenly lively.

In their warm front room
we talked an hour.
The photos on the wall
were of family and clan
with the haunting cheekbones
and brandy-rich skin tones
of our Dad.
Before we left
Harrison called me
in to the high tin-ceilinged kitchen.
From among figurines of red and yellow roosters,

on the fading drain board window sill
he brought down six pinto beans
he'd saved aside up there,
dry and smooth and marked
with lines like human faces,
he cradled these spirit companions
from the earth beneath his feet
held them out to show me in his tawny palm.
"Look," he said.

Still Not Far from Yasgur's Farm

There are words that have magic sown into their fibers
that when uttered into sound,
spoken, set free to travel in the sea of air,
release the enchantment.
In my life and times that word is "Woodstock."

It thrums when spoken, usually at the end of a sentence
with an exclamation and expulsion of breath
that requires a rise in tone
and flourish of presentation.

The word is me at age 19, reeling from a breakup,
the summer after my first year at college,
with one foot at home
the rest of me exploring the universe
of psychedelia, Buddhism,
revolutionary politics.

Determined enough to get on a Trailways bus
ride all night to meet a friend with a car at Grand Central Station,
travel up to Bethel, leave the car about five miles from the site,
walk in, clutching an extra work shirt,
a bag of carrots and a floppy felt hat.
The awe of Yasgur's Farm,
when first coming around the bend in the road
and the whole site visible and audible
in teeming color in front of us.

Masses of youth, like me,
and all the music we could ever dream of.
Live. In front of us. Free.
Stretched out on the ground,
on a small plaid blanket
under the big open sky
sun music, dark music, moon music,
rain music, mud music…dancing, up all night music.

The word reminds me
that all of humanity is a one-celled organism
because I had never known that
before being and breathing there.

I still know that truth.

This was the birth of a self who is still me.

I could have not been anywhere else,
the beginning of the peak of my independence,
and I sucked it in like the drag from my first joint,
passed to me by a stranger, passed by me to a stranger
and all half-million strangers
were my best friends.

The Apprentice Plumber Walks Home from Trade School

Pale rose light behind the bud bare branches,
I walk down 16th Avenue
around stubborn sidewalk snow
hard as concrete, gray and gritty
with trickle floes of melt beneath,
working their way to the gutter.

My mind is full of angles, offset equations,
getting home from trade school,
and the moon-eyed carpenter
studding walls on our job
this morning.

The massive apartment building
where I live stands like a day's end Dobbin,
ancient, content and steady,
the huge front windows
his eyes, half-lidded now
against the evening's pinkish light.

I am a workhorse, too
in this city alone four years,
with jobs that take all of me
out of me.
Breathing in deeply,
I steep in my solitude.

Home by just-dark
I stand at my kitchen window,
sipping tea for
the rise of Orion.
I need a caring hand
to curry me and pat my head
when we lie on the rooftop
looking at stars.

Building: Denver, 1980s

My job, construction of
booming oil buildings
starting in a sewer ditch,
quickly graded, but right—
one-eighth inch the foot.

                        Large pipe fittings that lie on
                        their backs, looking up,
                        allowing vertical risers
                        up out of the ground,
                        ten feet at a time—

we plumbers smacking spigot ends,
smeared with lube,
into cast iron hubs
with chain pullers until
they popped home—true.

I loved the logic of the systems,
waste, vents, storm and water
the beautiful plane geometry of clean
new lines, perfectly hung, coaxed
aside if needed and aligned plumb,
level or graded, hung effortlessly,
almost daintily,
from three-eighths, one-half,
or five-eighths inch all-thread rod,
or chocked on the horizontal
tamped, new-dug dirt to hold grade.
Shiny stainless nuts and washers
by the box for hanger making.

I could create something
pretty from these stray pieces
riding home deep in my
bib pockets. Electrician's wire
spoke to me as earrings,
twisted colors in fine,
soft turns and knotted designs.

                        Each craft on site,
                        a different color hard hat

We were purple, plumbers and pipefitters,
half-siblings, sometimes sharing
work, always fighting over welding.
                      Ironworkers, brown, men half-crazy climbing
crane-swinging steel, cold pointed chisels and rivet
pouches for gear fastened and hanging from wide
leather waist belts.
Better to be out of the ditches
days they were there.
One told me he could become
a bird high on the skeleton
when the wind came strong.
This birdman wore a diamond stud
earring that easily caught the sun.
I imagined when he flew,
the diamond would wink at me,
toiling far below in the muddy sewer trench.
       Waves of form-setting carpenters,
    blue hats, early on, cocky and smart-ass loud.
                One job, bricklayers, white hats, for weeks, their
hod carrier running
loads in a cat supplying five or six troughs along
their curving, spidery scaffold.
In constant motion, the huge guy,
his name was Rose, took to me and
bellowed a name he made for me each time
he passed, wheeling by
as I carried 20 foot lengths of copper pipe or
a Prest-O-Lite bottle on my shoulder,
through the mud from the tool trailer.

                "Looper!" Rose yelled at me,
his toothy satchel-mouth smile
made me blush, eyes downward,
because I did not know what he meant by that
name.

                An old plasterer
his stance perpendicular to
his convex wall
held a big plywood palette,

like an oil painter,
his local down to seven members,
theirs a lost craft,
replaced by drywall.

Back from Vietnam,
the younger guys built nuke plants
in the early 70s.
They told travel stories of being
on the road for months,
in windy places like Cheyenne
or vast sites outside holes of towns
in Montana or the Dakotas.
They chased the welding jobs,
government power plants of miles
of stainless steel pipe.
They crafted
belt buckles from
bias-cut ovals of the precious, shiny stuff,
finding ways to hide away all day
in the newly-born bowels
rising out of the flats, lonely and pancake-plain.

The only woman on the job site,
I heard their rough songs, those men,
from a distance.

One afternoon I hiked out
past our old pipe boneyard to see the building
from that new elevation.
Due west of the job,
a hundred yards or so tucked alongside
the first foothill, invisible
beyond the reeds and rushes,
a small pond more long than wide.
There I saw my first pair
of wood ducks. They floated in complete
colorful serenity, the drake's head
muted rust and vibrant turquoise,
a splotch of yolk yellow across his wing.

Their calm held me
past the shabby pinewood pallets of
banded sanitary pipe fittings
and blue ductile iron flanged valves.
I carried this close when I walked back
to the job, like company, like peace,
stuck deep in my pockets.

In and Out of the Horse Latitudes

I could see the coal on the map
before we moved here,
in the stacked-up, convoluted lines
folding in on themselves along the Alleghenies,
running counter to the rest of the land,
where the thick green brush of outspoken woody forests
died to give way to the smudgy bituminous stuff,
its next incarnation.

In 1987, we moved to this hard, poor land
with our good intentions,
a will to love each other, and less than $150.
In an upstairs apartment one block from the Goodwill
we entered the horse latitudes of our time together:
no work, no car, burned bridges between here and our last state.

My boyfriend settled to slip deeper into his addictions,
revolutionary politics and pills,
leaving me to take hold, dig in,
learn the lay of this sorry land alone
and find work.

A backward Baptist God blessed
this place with humidity, humbling us all
to free the gung-ho from our Northern natures,
like a slow leak from an overblown balloon.
By August we knew we'd not survive together.
He packed a few spare boxes,
sent them UPS on borrowed funds,
and headed back to the West coast.

The irresistible land became my new love,
and waited out the time for me
with its thick-waisted, ancient hills
red-orange, then brown and green
and the spooky mist, translucent, smoky-white
rising off all morning, every morning.

I worked hard, healed and scraped bottom
like never before in West Virginia, using all
fingers and toes to clear the gravelly

surface, push in my single seed
and say "home."

My River Life

The muddy Elk flows to its end
in the armpit of the waters of the Great Kanawha
in Charleston's old Westside neighborhood
where I lived on the second floor—a flat
in a 1920's era brick building.
Four rooms lay in a line
heated by squatty gas stoves
hunched on the tiled hearths
one in the first room,
the other in the bedroom.
I stuffed newspapers in the gaps
around the windows
to stifle the draft in winter,
wedged fans in the open window space
in summer, to draw in and move
the sultry West Virginia air.

Home from hoot owl shift
at the boiler house
I slept with the yellow foam plugs
stuffed deep down in my ears,
in my window shaded room
that hung over Tennessee Avenue.
I felt my building shiver
when semis crossed the interstate bridge:
our structures married below
to the same family of bedrock.

I had never before lived so close to a river.
In sleep I rode its current,
taken away by its ancient flow.
I knew on some level,
maybe only in my dreams,
that this could drown another girl,
a lesser swimmer,
one afraid to face downstream.
I decided I would float,
I would swim.

The Language of Men

I claimed
what my Mother called
the language of men
to grind out my path
through life:
double-nutted,
leveled-up, balls-
to-the-wall sounds
that speak of tools, machines,
equipment, of picks
and shovels,
of plumbing, boiler clinkers
and slag heaps,
fly ash and bottom slurry;
of leverage, alignment and
elevations, slab on grade
foundations, risers, and
vent stacks.

Sounds with
strong constitutions and
bellies full of beer;
sure footed,
cramped on to the bottoms
of their lug sole boots,
spat out with
chew juice, wry smiles
and an outbreak of
swearing.

I found my life
within the close and
crumbly walls of
a six-foot ditch,
opened raw this morning,
riding cast
iron ponies and shin-scraping
lining bars breathing freshly
pulverized coal and its heat
that felt like the breath
of a familiar monster,

or the left eye
of shame.

I took time in the
heaving rafters of the
powerhouse past midnight,
to catch and count my breath,
to face the woman I wasn't sure I knew.
I was lonely in the roar and hiss
in the womb of continual labor.
I owned the words
that had no such meaning.

Poem Inspired by James Wright's Fear of Working in the Glass Plant

I was in your factory,
not glass but chemicals,
the steam plant, midnight shift.
I close my eyes and see black rail cars
awash in the weak light
like massive open caskets full of coal
pulled under the boiler house
with their lush cargo offered up
to the curling licks of hungry fire
the bulging pipes carried steam
rushing at the pressure of 600 pounds
from boilers to generators
and out to various headers—
every other location in the factory
depended on the steam we made.

I came here because I could
after a short career laying track
and ten years plumbing in Colorado,
this was the best job in the valley,
pay-wise. Everyone said if you got on at Carbide
You were set. For life.
I doubted I would live that long.
I loved the work itself, the dimension and force of it,
burning carbon from deep in the ground to boil water
from the ancient river,
then containing the resulting power to create sophisticated products,
coatings, gums, surfactants…
The work gave me satisfaction and physical ails
along with a growing bank account
but my separation and loneliness grew.
Many nights I slipped into the locker room between my rounds
with a paperback book shoved down the front of my coveralls
I lay flat on the long wood bench
between the rows of lockers,
finding comfort in the words.

Escaping the heat, outside on the catwalk,
above the Great Kanawha River,
I sat behind the shadows of the smokestacks
in the blessed midnight air.

The sparse lighting of the grated walkways
clinging to the outside of the building
looked like starlight:
each globe shaded with a covering of coal dust,
like my sweaty face and arms.

Walking home at six am,
across the Patrick Street bridge
I looked back
to imagine a sudden inferno uncontained
swallowing it all up,
setting me free.
Yeah, James, some mornings,
I burned it all down.

My Coat with Rainbow Sleeves

I pick up the many partial skeins of yarn around my house
to knit a coat that is the story of my life
the best way I can tell it.

I make no attempt to bind dropped stitches from unravelling,
they are my ragged reflection, my stubborn stand-in
for beauty.

The big hole in my center is where my unnamed baby,
given up, fell through, roughly pulling pieces
of my body's stuffing out with him.

The sleeves are rainbows
miles long, and wide as sunrise.
Their colors paint my portrait,
my flushed rose cheeks and blue bruised lips
memories of black cherry blood;
the ochre and cream of innocence,
like the shades of a daisy chain that was my childhood,
green ache of first love
and the depths of purple pain.

Some mornings I pull the ample collar
over my head and walk faceless
into town.

Far from Home

I know the light this evening
blue-gray, a rainy egg-wash
muting the September dusk.
I sit in my truck
waiting out a rain storm,
with a load of tools and blueprints.
I observed my crew repair a gas line,
I am the Compliance Officer,
the deliverer of the regulations
that direct our workday.
I share them with the men
with the backhoe and picks and shovels
and knowledge of how to deftly expose
the pressurized lines that sometimes hide
beneath several feet of West Virginia clay.

They've finished but I sit and stare
at the dwellings, the outcrop of wealth
in this suburb where houses are too big,
massive brick showplaces with complicated rooflines
and multiple bedrooms.

I see my Grandmother
from years before this,
in another quiet brick abode, in another city, another state,
taking an umbrella from the master as he enters
and placing it open to dry on the patio
covered with ivy and lilacs.
Quickly, she passes to the kitchen
to help her cousin Helen serve soup
to the children at their table.
I see her in deft anticipation
of their need before they want it,
her quiet skill of nonintrusion.

Now I imagine what the silence would be like
upstairs inside those extra bedrooms.
Even at this distance
I feel the solid, hollow vacuum.
What Grandma surely felt,

in a strange huge house miles from the familiarity
of her father's close, simple home on the reservation.

Out here on the street,
generations away from her quiet step
through rich people's homes,
I, too, am here when they call me,
here to serve with a skillful response
that renders me invisible.

Her loneliness swallows me whole.

Mary Imo-Stike was born and raised in Rochester, NY.

Travelling after college, she landed in Denver, Colorado and spent ten years there, working as a rail worker and then a union plumber.

The hills of West Virginia called out to her, and she answered by moving to Charleston in 1987. There she worked as a boiler operator at a large chemical plant, where she also had jobs as a training specialist, and an environmental technician. She also spent time at an oil and gas facility, employed as a Compliance Officer.

When retired from work-life, Mary obtained an MFA in Poetry from West Virginia Wesleyan College in 2015.

Her poems tell her story of growing up in the 1950s and 60s, reflecting on her childhood family life and stories; her awareness of the lack of opportunities faced by her native grandmother and other kin on the reservation, her debt to the legacy of both of her grandmothers' attitudes toward work; and memories of some defining moments of those times: the race riots of the 1960s, and the Woodstock Festival.

They are inspired by seeing herself as a pioneer on the front lines of the second wave of the Women's Liberation Movement by working at her non-traditional jobs.

Mary was the poetry co-editor of *HeartWood*, the online literary magazine of West Virginia Wesleyan College and is co-creator of More Than Words* a monthly literary event featuring presentations by West Virginia writers in her community of Hurricane, WV.

She shares a quiet home life with her husband John and their much-loved canine Howie.

www.ingramcontent.com/pod-product-compliance
Lightning Source LLC
LaVergne TN
LVHW041601070426
835507LV00011B/1240